The Eruption
Jacqueline James

The Eruption
Jacqueline James

Published By Parables
February, 2020

All Rights Reserved. No part of this book may be reproduced or utilized in any form or by any means, electronic or mechanical, including photocopying, recording, or by any information storage and retrieval system, without permission in writing from the author.

Unless otherwise specified Scripture quotations are taken from the authorized version of the King James Bible.

Readers should be aware that Internet Web sites offered as citations and/or sources for further information may have been changed or disappeared between the time this was written and when it is read..

ISBN 978-1-951497-26-2   Copyright by Jacqueline James

Illustration provided by www.unsplash.com

The Eruption
Jacqueline James

PUBLISHED by PARABLES
Earthly Stories with a Heavenly Meaning

Table of Content.

General   7
   1. What Makes...   9
   2. Give My Life Back...   10
   3. Life Transformation...   11
   4. I Cried...   12
   5. My Granddaughters...   13
   6. Me...   14
   7. Meeting New Friends...   15
   8. The Invitation...   16
   9. That's it...That's all...   17
   10. It's Real..   18

Spiritual   21
   1. Grateful...   22
   2. Glorious...   23
   3. My "Angel"...   24
   4. But God…   25
   5. Second Prayer..   26.
   6. Third Prayer...   28
   7 Repent...   29
   8. Jesus in Prayer...   30
   9. Get out of God's Way...   31
   10. Pray for the Children...   32

Educational   35
   1. Secrets...   36
   2. Absent Dad...   37
   3. Work it Out...   39
   4. Our Fight...   40
   5. Humiliated...   42
   6. Violated...   43

Informative   43
    1. Enriched...   46
    2. I Know...   48
    3. Souls...   49
    4. The Graduates...   51
    5. My Grandmother, My Grandmother...   52
    6. Reunite...   54
    7. The Healthy Patient...   55
    8. Double-dipping...   56
    9. The Audience...   58

Entertainment   59
    1. It's Hot...   60
    2. Leasing Life...   61
    3. Weeble Wobble...   63
    4. Little Baby...   64
    5. I'm 23...   66
    6. They Tripped...   67
    7. Rock Stable...   69
    7. Time Out...   71
    9. Money...Money...   73
    10. Party...   75
    11. Me Time...   77
    12. In the...   78
    13. Spicy Seniors...   79
    14. Old Folks...   81

Special Dedication   83
    1. Time to Heal...   84
    2. Gone Home...   85
    3. The King Called Me Home...   87
    4. Liked Spirits...   89
    5. R.I.P...   90

About the Author

Jacqueline James is a very talented devoted Christian who is family oriented. She is also a charismatic poetess and published author who shares her special talent in this book.
Jacqueline will allow you to embrace her sensitive side, as she graciously invites you into her personal world. God's gift of writing, expressed through her poetry is where she finds her pleasure. Through Jacqueline's creativity, she has written other astonishing books to explore. Other books include, "Poetry with a Twist," "The Spiral Affect," "Let it Overflow,"and "X-pression," all of which are completely categorized books of poetry, containing several inspiring poems. Jacqueline's mission is to allow her audience (you) to share her divine passion and from it be blessed throughout your life endeavours.

The Dedication

This book "The Eruption," is dedicated to my son Charles Unique Buchanan.

Charles has overcome very challenging obstacles in his life. With courage and perseverance he has defeated all odds stacked against him, for that I greatly admire him. Over the years life has thrown him lemons, and I had the privilege of watching him diligently make lemonade from them. Charles is a very confident, intelligent, dependable, and hard working person, with a heart of gold. He has a great passion for his work as an activist for equal rights, civil rights, and the rights for all human beings. All of this work makes him a true humanitarian. Charles has proven himself to be effective and essential and overall a stand up guy. He is greatly respected and appreciated among his circle of peers for the persistence and courage he continuously demonstrates through his leadership qualities.

I specifically chose this particular book, "The Eruption," as a metaphor to describe certain characteristics that Charles possesses. Similar to the beauty of a volcano erupting hot lava from its contents melting everything in his path, it reminds me of the strength Charles relentlessly determinations. He has the qualities of a true warrior, never ceasing until his path has been cleared of all negativity and situations have resolved in a favorable manner. When circumstances became difficult he didn't give up, instead he pushed harder through the worst, and evolved into a better, stronger person.

Charles, I am very proud of you, and I truly value all the things that I have learned from you over the years. Continue to follow your heart's desire and to fight for what you believe in with strong conviction. Charles, always remember never to accept more than

THE ERUPTION

you're willing to give. Take the time out to laugh, have a picnic, walk the dog, speed on the highway, play in the rain, read all of Mamas books, and most of all remember to love yourself as much as you love others. I love you Charles, and I thank God for choosing me to be your mother. You're the most "Unique" blessing He has bestowed upon me.

Introduction

"The Eruption," was creatively designed to enhance your perspective and the way that you view everyday encounters. This book contains very impressive reading material, written by the talented poetess, Jacqueline James. You will be able to identify with her passion when you read these remarkable poems. The author meticulously chose several authentic poems from her collection to be published in this particular book. This will give you an opportunity to indulge in pleasurable reading time.

The ways you respond to different circumstances were taking in consideration by the author as she carefully categorize each section of this book. Jacqueline's objective was to comfortably introduce you to different levels of understanding through her poems. Jacqueline intentions are to enlighten your awareness on some sensitive subjects while she entertains you in the process. After reading this book you'll find a sense of fulfilment from your most simplest to challenging moments and be comforted by the authors words of endearment. So, make some time to relax, unwind, and enjoy a few of the finest pieces of Jacqueline's work.

Thank You

I thank God for the enriched thoughts that He has planted in my mind expressed through the poetry written in each of my books. May He continued to bless me and to bless others through my writing.

I would like to express my sincere gratitude for the love and support that my daughter Jeannie Davis has given me during this process. Jeannie I truly appreciate all of your hard work and the countless effort that has gone into helping me with this project.

I also thank my readers, as well as my fans for continuing to purchase my books. I truly appreciate each one of you for your support.

A special thanks to my mother, Jeannette Whitehorn for always being my "biggest fan."

I thank each of my children, Sherece Whitehorn, Cedric Haynes, Charles Buchanan, Centilus Buchanan, and Lee James. Also a big thanks to each of my grandchildren. My family have all been my motivation inspiring me to continue to write.

Chapter 1
General

1. What Makes...
2. Give My Life Back...
3. Life Transformation...
4. I Cried...
5. My Granddaughters...
6. Me...
7. Meeting New Friends...
8. The Invitation...
9. That's it...That's all...
10. It's Real...

THE ERUPTION

What Makes...

What makes you live, can make you die;
Or maybe just sit down and cry,
When you look back on what you had;
It can make you happy, or make you sad,
You might wonder what would've been;
If only you did things differently, way-back-when,
Even though we can't change our past;
It doesn't stop us from wanting to re-hash,
Our present times, may reflect;
On all the things we choose to neglect,
However, when were forced to hear;
We reminisce on things we once feared,
There's lots of times that we've grown to regret;
Nevertheless, our conscious wont allow us to forget,
Other times, we wish that we could have savoured;
Cause those were times that showed us favor,
We've all been drove down memory lane;
But all of our views haven't been the same,
Some of our memories were a big quest in life;
While others were a reason to fight,
Whatever road we chose to take;
We've made it through for heaven's sake,
So, the next time we reflect on our past;
Don't get hung up on what didn't last;
Embrace your presence as of now;
And prepare for the future and you'll be proud.

THE ERUPTION

Give My life Back……

Oh I'm crying out for room to breathe;
For my life, I beg you please,
Listen closely and you'll hear;
In my voice, you'll feel my fear,
Release me from your bitter hold;
In my days, I'll have control,
Give me back my proper place;
And there'll be a smile on my face,
I've been down, can't you see;
From the wicked things you've done to me,
Give me back my self-esteem;
After all, I'm a human being,
You strickened me from my earthy pride;
Leaving me feeling low inside,
You didn't allow me to have a say;
It left me with a hopeless day,
Remove me from this horrible sight;
So, once again, I'll see the light,
Let me see stars again;
And maybe you can be my friend.

JACQUELINE JAMES

Life Transformations...

Throughout our lives, we go through many transformations;
And were forced to develop new relations,
Sometimes were up and enjoying our success;
Other times were not and settling for less,
Nevertheless, we try our best;
To live and prosper, without any stress,
We all start off not knowing much;
When life hits us hard, we put up a fuss,
None of us in the beginning, really know;
We all must go through something, in order to grow,
We must take the bitter with the sweet;
There will always be life demands to meet,
If you approach things trying to avoid the obstacles in life;
Then you're in for challenges and you're up for a fight,
You must crawl before you walk, that's just the way it goes;
If you go up too fast, you're coming back down- you know,
So, work hard and satisfy your own situation;
And remember each one of us will go through life transformations.

THE ERUPTION

I Cried...

What you're sorry? Like you didn't hear me cry?
This time you can't make up for your lie!
I cried, you heard me, but you didn't answer;
I cried, louder, and harder; then it festered!
I cried, I was scared, but you heard;
I cried some more, you heard me, but ignore,
I cried, you were there, but not for me;
I cried, but you never even stop to see,
I cried, I was in pain, but it didn't matter to you;
I cried longer, you didn't come, you had other things to do,
I cried, I begged you to help me;
I cried, you never once said, "Let me be,"
I cried again, and I cried again, and I cried so more;
I cried, you never even opened the door,
I cried for you, my life was in your hands;
I cried, hoping you'd understand,
I cried, wanting desperately to be at ease;
I cried, I didn't know that you were displeased,
I cried, I was hurting all over;
I cried, you were busy with your lover,
I cried, I just wanted some relief;
I cried, no answer, I was only left with grief.

My Granddaughters...

My granddaughters are a reflection of me;
They're dreams of what I wanted to be,
All the hope from my tender years;
When I was invincible without fear,
All the things that I pretended to be;
What I waited patiently for the world to see,
All of my youth capture through their beauty;
To give them the world, would be my duty,
I lavish over their wits and charm;
When I cradle them comfortably in my arms,
My granddaughters are very precious indeed;
When God gave them life, I was especially pleased,
All the talent they have within;
Lets me know in life, they'll win,
I love them both with all my heart;
I'll split it in half to do my part,
They're both from different walks of life;
However, I see myself when I hold them tight,
They're little "Angels from above;"
God has blessed me with their precious love.

THE ERUPTION

Me...

You might be able to suppress me;
But eventually you must address me;
Because I'm a different breed;
And I require different needs,
I'm not your average, nor do I fit in your "norm;"
However, my goal here is not to do you any harm,
To understand by nature, you need a different mind set;
Indulge yourself with possibilities you won't regret,
I am unique in every sense of the word;
With unimaginable qualities you haven't yet heard,
Give yourself a moment throughout time;
To appreciate the complexities of my kind,
Relax and roll with the flow;
You've come across a winner, didnt you know?
I'll rise above all of the unnecessary crap;
I'll work hard for the 1st, and you'll get what's left,
I'm always going to outshine the rest;
I'm better than "good stock," I am the best.

JACQUELINE JAMES

Meeting New Friends...

While on vacation, I met some friends that were kind;
And I'm truly grateful that they were willing to be mine:
They were people from all over the world;
And they grew fond of me, just a local town girl,
I shared with them some pleasant days;
By being subtle in my ways:
We had a lots of memorable times;
And I photographed them, to make them mine:
We ate good food, talked, and laughed together;
We shared our life stories through the sunny and rainy weather:
I didn't want my vacation to end;
However, I made some pretty cool friends.

THE ERUPTION

The Invitation...

It's one thing not to be invited to something;
And it's another thing to be invited but not welcome,
I was verbally invited to a party;
When I arrived I wasn't welcome, not hardly,
I wondered was it a waste of time on my part;
Or was it done intentionally from the heart,
So I stayed to mingle for a while;
Until I noticed I cramped their style,
I started to speak to see who would listen;
Then I was shown the invitation list and my name wasn't mentioned,
Then I regained my composure and headed for the door;
But as I started to exit it began to pour,
So, then I pause to see if anyone cared;
But they were adamant; they made things clear,
So I looked around to find the jerk who invited me;
He was across the room chuckling in spite of me,
Shame was covered across my face;
And I knew at that moment I had to leave that place,
So I hurried out, rain or not;
And found my car on the parking lot.

That's it... That's all...

That's it, that's all!
Socially awkward you need to make that call,
You don't fit in; you need a friend;
Or some personality, I'm willing to lend,
You're loud and obnoxious everywhere;
And you're very rude and dont even care,
You always want to be seen, but you're hard to miss;
You draw attention to yourself then try to "dis,"
The time I spend with you is just wasteful,
And the company you choose, are very distasteful,
Your very presence makes things complicated;
Because you're not loyal or dedicated,
You're constantly bringing up things from my past;
And, that's weird, cause I didn't even know you, yet you're talking trash,
You're trying to judge me, but you don't have the right;
Instead of going to sleep, you're up arguing all night,
You're very annoying and just plain nerve-wrecking;
I want you gone, so can you please start packing?
I have nothing left to say, my back is up against the wall;
So I need you to know, thats it... and that's all!

THE ERUPTION

It's Real...

What you want, I can't give;
Because you want something that you can feel;
And as of now, I'm keeping it real;
So I'm going to sit back and chill,
While you go looking for a cheap thrill;
I'm praying that you don't get killed,
I hope that you know the deal;
This crap out here is for real!
Make sure the deal is sealed;
Before you pay the bill,
Or you'll be up the hill;
Feeling real ill,
Listen up if you will;
You better keep still;
While you riding in your Seville;
Creeping past the mill,
With gold on your wheels;
Trying to find a girl named Jill;
who's willing to kneel,
After you take the little blue pill;
And you're not going to yield,
Because you have too much zeal!

JACQUELINE JAMES

THE ERUPTION

Chapter 2
Spiritual
1. Grateful...
2. Glorious...
3. My Angel...
4. But God...
5. Second Prayer...
6. Third Prayer...
7. Repent...
8. Jesus in Prayer...
9. Get Out of God's Way...
10. Pray for the Children...

THE ERUPTION

Grateful...

I'm grateful to serve in Jesus name;
Without His words through me; my life wouldn't be the same
God has touched me in such a remarkable way;
And I'm grateful for everything I do and say,
God gives me strength, throughout my fight;
I only breathe through Jesus' light,
I sometimes face difficult times;
However, through God's grace, victory is mine,
I'm grateful to see another day;
As I kneel I start to pray,
I thank Him for the things He's done;
How He sent His only begotten son,
How He loved me first and die for me,
He forgave my sins and set my soul free,
I'm grateful for Jesus' love from day to night
I thank Him for sending me messages as I write,
I'm grateful for all the blessings that He gives;
And a faithful and Christan life I'll live,
I'm grateful for his mercy and his grace;
I'll live righteously until I see my father's face,
I'm grateful for the way he makes me feel;
I'll show humility as I live,
I'm blessed and highly favored,
And for that I'm truly grateful.

Glorious...

I was created to be glorious,
My Lord and Savior died to bring out the joy in us,
I do believe with strong conviction;
That I will prosper and rise above all restrictions,
I will succeed without limitations;
Because of my faith and my dedication,
I am totally committed to my work and thoughts;
Because my Lord and Savior brought me out;
I'm in perfect harmony with my Lord;
My days are not stressful, nor are they hard,
"His will" be done in my day;
Because of His grace He has His way,
He keeps my spirit in perfect peace;
Because of His love my faith increase;
My life today is glorious;
And His gift through me means so much;
The world must see it in magnitude;
How he humbly changed my attitude,
I was created to serve The King at all expense;
And live righteous and be content,
I was created through time and passage;
To bring the world a glorious message.

My Angel...

Throughout my days God sends me an angel;
To protect me from any harm or danger,
They watch me carefully to make sure its cool;
So that no one is bothering me, or being rude,
The hands that serve me are very blessed;
This prevents me from going through any stress,
My angel may come in the form of a stranger;
But I believe In my heart I'm in no danger,
I might be stranded on the road;
But God will send me an angel so I'm not left alone in the cold,
I may be hungry, in need of some food;
But, I'll get a call from an angel with good news,
When my bills are due and there's not enough money;
God sends my angel and my day becomes sunny,
I might be scared and in despair;
But when I see an angel and know Gods near,
I may have a problem carrying out my daily plan;
However, God will send an angel to help me understand,
And because I pray my faith is strong;
And God know what's best; he's never wrong,
I thank God for all He does for me;
He truly protects me, as you can see.

JACQUELINE JAMES

But God...

God is anywhere you want him;
And is everywhere you need him to be,
I thank you God for watching over me,
He kept me safe through my storm;
No weapon formed did me harm,
Now the peace of mind that I've formed;
Is because I'm cradled in His arms,
My life today is satisfied;
Because He hung his head and died,
He didn't have to save a ranch like me;
But because He did my soul is free,
Now I'm able to understand,
To live as a Christian is His perfect plan,
God will be with you in your time of need;
He died for our salvation this you must believe,
If you talk to God when you're hurt;
You'll see how his love truly works,
He understands what you're going through;
He'll help you and deliver you,
When everyone else turns their back;
God stays with you and that's a fact,
So while you're going through your fight;
Just look up and you'll see Jesus' light,
He'll relieve any and all of your pain;
You'll be at peace in Jesus name.

THE ERUPTION

Second Prayer...

I came to a place in its darkest hour,
It was in desperate need of the Holy Ghost Power,
I drop to my knees and began to pray;

"Please Lord listen to want I have to say,
Hear my cry, my Lord and Savior;
I beg of you to show me favor!
I need your help and that's no doubt;
Cause your love, I can't live without,
Give me strength in my time of need;
It's your word I long to receive,
Order the steps that's right for me;
Make me righteous, so my soul is free,
Cradle me safely in your arms;
Let no weapon formed against me do me no harm,
Shelter me from the wicked ones;
Keep me quiet through my storm,
Keep my spirit raging with your peace;
Help my faith in you increase,
Always give me a song to sing;
Filled with the love and mercy you bring,
Give me sight to admire your beauty;

Jacqueline James

As a Christian I'll do my duty,
Before I return, back to the dirt;
Show the world that your blood still works,
Thank you Jesus for all the above;
I'm blessed to receive your love."

THE ERUPTION

Third Prayer...

I pray every night like there's no tomorrow;
I pray for joy and peace in the midst of my sorrow,
I have a little talk with Jesus in the middle of the night;
He reassures me that everything's going to be alright,

"Bless me Lord as I call your name;
Come into my heart, don't leave me the same,
Keep my mind stayed on you,
When I pray, I'll know what's to do,
I'm awake writing through the night;
Because of your grace I feel alright,
People see me shout and think that I'm in distress;
No I shout with joy because I'm truly blessed,
They even hand me a tissue to wipe my face;
But there's no tears, I'm full of grace,
They don't understand that the love you give,
Keeps me happy through the days I live,
If they wanna know about your Holy Ghost Power;
They need to see me dance throughout the hours,
Yes, I'm different and I know that;
Cause I'm living for Jesus and that's a fact!
When you look at me then you'll see;
A reflection of Jesus shining through me,
Thank you Jesus for all that you do,
Keeping me safe and peaceful too!"

Repent...

It's good to go to confession;
If you truly learnt your lesson,
However, if you're a repeat offender;
Then you need Jesus, cause you're a sinner,
Don't be fooled or deceived;
That's why He died, you must believe,
To forgive us is why Jesus was sent;
So you need to confess, then repent,
You must live your life for Jesus;
He died for that very reason,
Give Him your all-and-all;
Jesus is the name you can always call,
He'll be there for you until the end;
And He'll forgive you for all your sins,
So, give Him a chance if you may;
He'll be with you when you pray,
You must be willing to do your part;
And allow Jesus to come into your heart;
It must be done by your free will;
And a righteous life you'll live,
Accept Jesus as your personal savior;
And with His grace He'll show you favor,
Now you must repent to make it right;
And you'll be blessed to see God's light.

THE ERUPTION

Jesus in Prayer...

We all have a cross to bare;
Don't you doubt that Jesus cares,
The devil is watching, so be aware;
And he's trying to destroy you, when he's near,
He comes in all shapes and sizes;
He'll jump into the ones you love, so don't be surprised,
He's busy trying to steal your soul;
But, if you allow Jesus in He'll take control,
He'll be there for you day and night;
Through praise and prayer it'll be alright,
When you worship Our Father above;
He'll show you unconditional love,
He'll keep you peaceful, when it's time to fight;
The Holy Spirit will guide you to Jesus' light,
You'll be protected through difficult times in life;
God makes your experiences turn out right,
Through God's mercy, you'll be filled with joy;
He extends His love to every woman, man, girl, and boy,
So, next time when you're feeling low;
To Jesus in prayer is where you need to go.

Get Out of God's Way...

After we worship and pray;
We need to get out of God's way,
We need to let God take control;
If you have faith, he'll deliver your soul,

"We are your sheep when we're awake and asleep;
You are our shepherd that allows us to conquer, and defeat,
I'm fully committed to follow you Jesus anywhere;
I trust you completely with my care,
Jesus my life is in your hands;
And I'm willing to accept your commands,
Lead me where I need to be;
I'll always follow you faithfully,
Help me to understand your will;
So, I'll humbly serve you as I live,
Teach me the right things to say;
So, I'll be blessed throughout the day;
Order my steps closer to you;
Through your grace I'll know what to do,
Please Lord take charge of me;
Remove my shackles and set me free,
Help me Jesus stay out your way;
So I'll be called to meet the Father one day."

THE ERUPTION

Pray for the Children…

Pray for the children, they are in need;
They're seeing the world's lust and greed,
Pray for the children, for they are up late;
Seeing the world's violence and hate;
Pray for the children, satan has them in his hold;
He's trying to steal their joy and destroy their souls,
Pray for the children, they are without,
Faith in Jesus to bring them out,
Pray for the children, for they are confused;
They haven't read about Jesus' good news,
Pray for the children, help them please?
No one has showed them how to pray on their knees,
Pray for the children, for they are lost;
They don't know that Jesus paid their cost,
Pray for the children, show them the way;
They don't know their Savior was born on that holy day!
Pray for the children, help them believe;
The Holy Ghost is what they need to receive,
Pray for the children, give them hope;
Teach them that faith in Jesus will help them cope,
Pray for the children, "sing with them praise."
So they'll be blessed throughout their days,
Pray for the children, day and night;
So that they'll know about Jesus' light;
Pray for the children so they may live;

And believe through Jesus stripes they are healed,
Pray for the children, so they may try;
To work hard for deliverance before they die,
Pray for the children, teach them to obey;
Teach them to humble themselves and pray,
Pray for the children, that they may feel;
Jesus' love and mercy that he gives,
Pray for the children so they may know;
Jesus will be with them wherever they go,
Pray for the children, help them see the battle is won;
And to get to God, they must go through His son.

THE ERUPTION

Chapter 3
Educational
1. Secrets...
2. Absent Dad...
3. Work it Out...
4. Our Fight...
5. Humiliated...
6. Violated...

THE ERUPTION

Secrets...

When you're doing deeds that are morally forbidden;
You need to know "behind closed doors,"
doesn't make them hidden,
The things you've said and done have come to pass;
But your dirty secrets will never last,
You shut out others trying to be discreet;
While you violate the ones who are vulnerable and weak,
"Whatevers done in the dark will eventually come to the light,"
Because they come out later does not make it alright,
You'll reap what you sow and that's a proven fact;
While you are masquerading around and putting on an act,
You may fool some people by changing your style;
But the lies you told will only last for awhile,
The wrong you've done and the mischief you've chosen;
You better know it's going to be exposed,
The pain cuts real deep when it comes out later;
It evolves into a disaster or something greater,
Secrets whispered by night then revealed in the day;
Now the world is wondering what you had to say.

Absent Dad...

I raised my kids all by myself;
With the grace of God I didn't need your help,
Now you wanna give me grieve;
And bad mouth me when you speak,
You didn't see our struggle you were never there;
However you walk around boasting as if you care,
You said that you were busy doing you!
But you had children and obligations too,
Their childhood was happy and filled with love;
They were highly favored from our Father above,
Over the years I spend time teaching them;
Nourishing them;
Feeding them;
Playing with them;
Caring for them;
Loving them;
And always praying with them and praying for them,
They were taught at an early age;
How Jesus' love would bless their days,
Now you want to play a parent it's much too late,
Their all grown up and turned out great,
They worked hard for all of their accomplishments;
From perseverance their success' were astonishing,

THE ERUPTION

And if you're not proud of them to say it out loud;
Then you need to keep-it-moving along with the crowd,
We don't have time for your negativity;
We're all about the positive energy,
Now I'm asking you nicely to step out of their way;
And if you want to get to know them, then you need to go to
Church and pray!

Work it Out...

Work with the cards that you were given;
Because Jesus is the reason that we're all living,
Accept the things that's rightfully yours;
And please don't expect anything more,
Take advantage of the things that are yours and don't hesitate;
Be willing to strive and participate,
Give life your best and sacrifice;
There is no need to do things twice,
You may not have what you see others with;
But there's no need for you to quit,
We're all here through time for a season,
So find your purpose and know your reason;
Come to Jesus and give him your all;
He's always here to answer your call,
Trust the response that he gives you;
Through faith you'll know the right thing to do,
Stay encouraged throughout your life;
Jesus will lighten the burden in your fight,
Focus on how greatly you're blessed;
then trust God to relieve all your stress.

Our Fight...

What do we expect to gain;
By reliving our same old pain?
Do you think its cool;
To see your enemies drool?
Our ancestors were all slaves;
Their blood paved our way,
Are we trying to let this generation see;
How they don't appreciate being free?
Are we trying to shame the white man;
From the brutally in their plan?
When we sing and bear our soul;
Do that makes us feel in control?
When we stop and tell our story;
Do you think they start to worry?
They degraded and raped our black women;
And they impregnated so many,
It changed the color of our skin;
Now we bear the white man's blood within,

Jacqueline James

A new generation of black people remains;
Leaving the white man to see his shame,
But where does that leave us;
Cultureless and filled with discuss,
We make up our own rules from the past;
Praying that the white man lies won't last,
We were denied the opportunity to read and write;
But that didn't stop us from our fight,
We're very intelligent race;
Despite of color of our face,
We battled many obstacles to gain our freedom;
Through dark places we've overcome,
We've overcome pain, abuse, and a whole lot more;
And now we're standing strong throughout our war,
The fight isn't over, there's more to come;
But by the grace of God our battles won.

THE ERUPTION

Humiliated...

Look right in front of you;
Guilt will be there waiting on you,
When you're ashamed of the things that you've said or done;
So you start to humiliate the ones you love,
You insult people for no reason and know it's wrong;
So don't expect their trust for long,
Your insecurities can get the best of you;
It'll affect the ones around you and they'll suffer too,
You don't regret the things you've done;
And you embarrass others just for fun,
All this pain is hurtful no doubt;
I'm trying to figure out what it's really about,
Are you just cold and calculating for no reason;
Or does your evilness come in seasons?
Why are you so bitter and mean;
Striking out at others like a bad dream?
In order to find some joy and peace;
All of this harshness has to cease;
You're going to be miserable by yourself;
With the nasty ways that you have left.

Violated...

When your innocence is snatched;
You're confused about the rest,
So you start to feel despair;
As if no one else cares:
Where were they when you were going through,
And you didn't know exactly what to do?
You were scared all the time;
About to lose your mind,
Your days were very long;
And you were left out on your own,
It wasn't your fault and you need to believe;
That you were violated and wrongfully deceived,
I'm sure you're hurting and very mad;
But you can't go through life feeling sad,
You must pull yourself together and move on;
Through faith in Jesus you'll grow strong,
It might be difficult to take my advice;
Because I know nothing about your life,
But I have Jesus' love that I'm willing to lead;
If you allow Him, He'll be your friend,
It might be hard to trust another;
When you were violated without your mother,
I know sometimes you may have to weep;
Because of the pain you buried deep,
Believe you're not by yourself;

THE ERUPTION

You have Jesus' love and his grace left,
Allow me, I'll be a comfort in your time of need;
And throughout life you will succeed,
We all have challenges to overcome;
When you're looking for mercy God is the one.

Chapter 4
Informative
1. Enriched...
2. I Know...
3. Souls...
4. The Graduates...
5. My Grandmother, My Grandmother...
6. Reunite...
7. The Healthy Patient...
8. Double-Dipping...
9. The Audience...

Enriched...

My heart is filled with content;
From the poems I wrote and the time I spent:
I am that star shining bright;
Pushing through dreams during the night:
The best that I have to offer you'll get;
From the depth of my soul the truth was sent:
Fill your mind with my thoughts;
If you're not inspired, it's not my fault:
I'll deliver unto you some clarity;
Then you can decide what you will see,
It's beyond reading when you hear my poems;
They'll filter through to my inner charm:
Brace yourself with all delight;
I'll take you to immeasurable heights:
If something sweet you haven't heard;
Then hold onto my every word,
The message is meant to enrich your life;
With a peace of mind you'll earn the right,
Now that I have your full attention;
You'll respect the things that I've chosen to mention,
Give yourself a moment to know;
And show some humility as you go,
I pray that your life will be enriched;
Filled with all the beauty and love that exist,

May all of your dreams come to pass;
With strong conviction they will last,
With an open door walk on through;
Claim the blessings that are meant for you,
You'll prosper greatly when you work hard;
And a successful life will be your reward.

THE ERUPTION

I Know...

I know everythings going to be fine;
Because all I do is speak in rhymes;
I know everythings going to be nice;
Because I write it once and read it twice,
I know everything is going to be alright;
Because I stay up working throughout the night,
I know everythings going to be neat;
Because the poems I write are very sweet,
I know everythings going to be mine;
Because the poems I write are one of a kind,
I know everythings going to be blessed;
Because God gives me the very best,
I know I'm going to live up to my every word;
Because Gods going to make sure my voice is heard,
I know everything is going to work in my favor;
Because of my time and my labour,
I know everythings going to be real good;
Because I pray and fast like I should,
I know everything brings hope to my days;
Because of my faithfulness and my praise,
I know everythings going to be great;
Because in Jesus is my faith;
I know for everything I'll give God the glory;
Because of his mercy I can tell my story.

Souls...

We can't choose who gets what soul;
You better know God is in control,
There may be an artist in a body without hands;
He uses his toes to meet the demands;
You call it a miracle I call it grace;
God is here during the challenges we face,

There may be a seamstress without fingers or toes;
However, she uses her tongue when she needs to sew,

Now there's a blind musician who can't see to read the notes;
However his ear are so keen he got an Oscar when they voted,
He plays the piano with great perfection;
His ears and hands make the connection,

Now there was a soul that when into a mentally challenged child;
She expresses her talent when she sings out loud,
She's capable of mimicking any voice she'd heard;
She sings with the harmony of a mockingbird,
Some calls it gifted I call it faith;
The God I serve doesn't make mistakes,

There was a man whose IQ made him retarded;
However through his accomplishments he was awarded,

THE ERUPTION

Some souls are given to babies hurting all over;
And they're sometimes abandoned by their fathers and mothers,
Some have sickness that makes them gasp for air;
Those souls were not given because God didn't care,
God knew exactly what to do;
He knows what's best for me and you,
All souls must pass through the challenges of time;
May it be a pianist, an author, a chemist, or mine,
Souls are given as a gift of life;
Jesus was born to save them all and his death paid their price.

JACQUELINE JAMES

The Graduates...

Proud and bold holding their own;
They graduated from college now they're grown,
We have to let them go to find their way;
They'll become future leaders one day,
They studied a lot in different varieties;
To become very successful in today's society,
They worked hard and made a pledge to commit;
When their struggle got intensed they didn't hesitate or quit,
With perseverance they pushed on through;
And now they see the world from a different view,
They found the courage in their heart;
To make wise choices from the start,
It took a lot of determination to overcome their odds;
And that alone made their parents proud,
Their accomplishments were well earned;
Because of the things they chose to learn,
They each chose their own career;
And completed it with confidence, not with fear,
Their determination helped them to succeed;
And with ambition they met their needs,
Now they have a degree and standing strong;
And with family support they are not alone,
This is the beginning of their success;
And they'll reach their destiny when they try their best.

THE ERUPTION

My Grandmother, My Grandmother...

My grandmother was particular and matter-of-fact;
She never let up and didn't give much slack,
She was swift with her tongue and had a potty mouth;
She was persistent, but she wasn't from down south,
She had the roar of a lion, but she wasn't very tall;
She was actually very tiny; I don't know how we listened at all,
When she was younger she ordered people around as if it were a game;
And when she got older she remained the same,
She got chauffeured around because she never learned to drive;
With this challenging world I don't know how she possibly survived,
However, she traveled abroad and even visit the White House!
And she explored with class as if she was the boss,
She got out a lot and did various things;
She was in the church choir and she even learn to sing,
When I came to visit she hardly took me outside;
We played indoor games and she baked apple pies,
She made homemade biscuits that were good to the taste;
But you had to eat them all, because she didn't like to waste,
She like to cook, but she didn't do it a lot;
She could show you what dieting was all about,

Jacqueline James

She was strong with discipline and even sometimes spanked;
But you better not pout, she expected to be thanked;
I used to sit on her stool where she would comb my hair;
And if I wiggle about she gave me quite a scare,
She made her children's clothing because she sewed very well;
And if they ripped them you better believe she yelled,
She had a loud barking dog that was really a pest;
She tried to train the dog to be quiet and she did her best,
I was very excited when I was old enough to drive her around;
Because this will be the day I was finally grown,
This was in the 80's when gas was a little over a buck;
If she paid me $0.50 it would be my luck,
Nevertheless I didn't mind doing it, in fact I was very proud;
Just to hear her give me the directions and say them aloud,
As time passed and her quality of life decreased;
She became homebound and her life photos brought her peace,
She lived a full life and I had the pleasure of taking care of her in the end;
She was much more to me than a grandmother,
she had become my friend.

THE ERUPTION

Reunite...

Seconds turn into minutes;
Minutes turn into hours;
Hours turn into days;
Days turn into weeks;
Weeks turn into months;
Months turn into years;
That's all I have left to hold back the tears,
It's impossible to know how to handle the unknown;
Always wondering, "Are you alone?"
Wanting to tell you, "Just be strong!"
The time is passing, it'll soon be gone,
The absence makes my heart aches;
Not being there for you as you wake,
My words can only describe how I feel;
Life wonders on to seal the deal,
Empty now, my heart and life;
I was your mother when I became his wife;
He had no right taking you away;
Leaving us both lonely throughout the day,
I just keep singing this same sad song;
Making my heart heavy as the day is long,
The time just passes but the pain won't leave;
We'll reunite soon I do believe.

JACQUELINE JAMES

The Healthy Patient…

All the doctors were amazed;
That the patient was healthy every day,
She's 76 years old;
And with a very spunky soul,
She was scheduled for a surgery;
But you had better believe I wasn't worried,
The doctors needed to get her personal information;
On her previous and present health situation,
She answered, "No" to all the questions that were asked;
And she laughed as she gave them the facts;
They were all a bit surprised;
To see that she was healthy and wise,
Then they prepped her for the surgery;
And one of the nurses escorted me to the waiting area,
Within 40 minutes,
The doctor came where I was sitting,
And told me he was finished;
He said that the surgery went well,
And that we could go because she's doing swell,
The doctor prescribed ointment and pills for the pain;
She said she'll use the ointment,
but he can keep the pills just the same,
All the doctors got a laugh;
And said she was the best patient that they have,
So I took her home; And she was back to herself before long.

THE ERUPTION

Double-Dipping...

Rapping, dancing, and singing like its no tomorrow;
Giving God the glory for your sorrows,
Worshipping on your knees,
praying for your sins throughout your day,
Stumping, pounding, and shouting out loud;
Just to look good before the crowd,
Hooping, hollering, and making noise;
Singing with the choir and singing until you're horse,
Fusing, fighting, up late at night;
That's all messed up, if you aint about that life,
Holding a Bible in one hand, and a beer in the other;
Going to church on Sundays, but laying up with your lover,
You were hanging out in the streets on Saturday nights making a mess of things;
And you're in church Sunday morning with no offering to bring,
Praising God, but cursing out your neighbor;
But you still want God to show you favor,
You want God to do something for you;
But you're unevenly yoked and still confused,
You're on your job keep it up sand;
Now you back in church lifting your hands,
You're going up and down the road preaching
to anyone who will listen;
However while you're quoting the Bible there's a few scriptures
you're missing,

Jacqueline James

You can only serve one master and that's a proven fact;
While you're out there partying Gods taking the slack,
You'll love one and end up hating the other;
But if you choose God a change will be coming,
However if you try to serve both your soul will be lost;
God will give you a reprobate mind because he's the boss!
And a fiery pit is where you'll be on your way;
Because you chose to party when it was time to pray,
You're double-dipping and your life isn't full;
It's very empty and your heart isn't pure.

THE ERUPTION

The Audience...

My audience is captivating, fascinating;
And very much appreciated,
I have a need to be filled like an itch that needs to be scratched;
And my audience must be that perfect match;
I've been holding back all my life;
I've always had a vision of expressing my talents in the light,
I've been praying for this opportunity;
It's on the way and it'll be new to me,
Nevertheless I'll get it right;
And the world will hear my voice from day to night;
I'm very confident just the same;
That everyone that hears will remember my name,
They're my audience for me to impress;
And because I'm grateful I'll give them my best,
I'll keep them longing for more to hear;
And pray that my message comes across clear,
I'll use this time so that they may understand my thoughts;
And they all appreciate what I'm really about,
For they are my audience and they've come to hear me;
I'll show them respect and they'll feel my humility,
They'll feel my spirit as I move the crowd;
And I give God the glory as I speak out loud!

Chapter 5
Entertainment
1. It's Hot...
2. Leasing Life...
3. Weeble Wobble...
4. Little Baby...
5. I'm 23...
6. They Tripped...
7. Rock Stable...
7. Time Out...
9. Money...Money...
10. Party...
11. Me Time...
12. In the...
13. Spicy Seniors...
14. Old Folks...

THE ERUPTION

Its Hot...

It was so hot outside I needed an umbrella to walk down the street;
I even got sick in the night's heat,
I was having an asthma attack before I made it to the corner;
The heat sucked my oxygen without any warning,
My mama ran off and left me, I thought she didn't love me;
But after I passed out then she decided to hug me,
We parked a block away just to save a dollar;
It was a park right next to the building,
but she didn't even bother to holler;
I was sweating so bad from my head to my toe;
I know next time I won't be going to that store,
I went through all of that for a thing of spice;
Hell, that trip nearly cost me my life,
I couldn't wait to get home at the end of the day;
I got central air and that's where I'm going to stay.

Leasing Life...

Wishing, hoping;
Smoking, coping;
Shouting, fighting;
Reading, writing;
Listening, learning;
Working, earning;
Practicing, teaching;
Praising, preaching;
Helping, having;
Joking, laughing;
Playing, teasing;
Taunting, pleasing;
Rapping, beating;
Killing, cheating;
Sexing, drugging;
Loving, hugging;
Sipping, spitting;
Peeping, sleeping;
Lying, creeping;
Robbing, stealing;
Touching, feeling;
Meeting, dating;
Talking, hating;
Finding, mating;
Rulings, rapping;

THE ERUPTION

Hunching, thumping;
Holding, humping;
Pipping, popping;
Stumping, stopping;
Looking, stalking;
Seeking, talking;
Wondering, waiting;
Digging, skating;
Wanting, needing;
Craving, feeding;
Watching, living;
Leading, giving;
Standing, moving;
Dancing, grooving;
Rolling, rocking;
Kicking, knocking;
Tipping, tapping;
Walking, stepping;
Swinging, ringing;
Crying, singing;
Dipping, dapping;
Snatching, grabbing;
Laying, staying;
Dying, praying.

Weeble Wobble...

Weeble wobble and I did fall down;
So much extra weight till I bounced off the ground:
I fell hard and landed on my knee;
And the black pavement covered with blood was the only thing I could see,
It was busted up pretty-badly and hurt like heck;
But I bounce back from all my fat:
I laid there 10 minutes trying to digest the pain;
And it was hurting so bad I wanted someone to blame:
The slippery shoes I wore it might've been that;
Or perhaps the uneven driveway that was filled with cracks:
And I try to get up and realize I couldn't stand on my own;
But in my left hand I was holding my phone:
So I called up my son embarrassed and all;
And asked him to please come over because I've just taken a fall:
It was a bit of a struggle, but he got me back onto my feet;
Then I limped into the house because my knee was weak:
So I looked at my scar and wiped it off clean;
It had swollen so large and I wanted to scream:
It could've been worse but nothing was broken;
So I stay in a hot tub with epsom salt soaking.

THE ERUPTION

Little Baby...

Little baby watch him lay;
Gently roll as he plays,
Up in the night, but sleep during the day;
Rapidly growing along the way,
Wanting to cherish these moments close;
Storing the memories for the most,
Watching him change before your eyes;
He's learning fast to your surprise,
Now he's noticing different things;
While he's rocking in his swing,
Everything he sees and hears is new,
He sits up wondering what to do,
He tastes the world with his mouth;
He wants to eat the toys you bought,
He's very cuddly, and very cute;
All dressed up in his little suit,
He'll crawl in the room and out the door;
So please make sure you mop the floor,
Now he's very busy all the time;
I hope you've read up on his kind,
He's discovering things all at once;
He even noticed he has a voice,
He yelled, and screams for want he wants;
And you jump through hurdles for every choice,
He no longer wants to sit on your lap;

Jacqueline James

Because he's taken his very first step,
Little baby on the run;
Oh so cute and so much fun!
Soon you'll see the time has passed;
Those precious moments will not last,
So hold him close while you can,
Before you know it, he'll be a man.

I'm "23"...

I'm 23,
What can you do for me?
Come on over let me see,
Or keep it movin and let me be,
I'm young, I'm cool, and I'm free;
You gotta be down for whatever to hang with me,
I'm on the move, I'm always on the go;
If you stop to think then you're kinda slow,
I talk real smooth and I'm pretty slick;
To catch my thoughts you have to be quick,
I always dress in the latest fads;
You're wearing last year styles now that's to bad,
My grip is tight; my styles are great;
And every time you see me I'm running late,
I have people to meet and places to go;
I can't hang out with you youngsters no more,
I'm important the world's waiting on me;
You better know this because I'm 23!

Jacqueline James

They Tripped...

This man has a wife and they have their own life;
I thought I had a man who had a good plan;
But I have a boy whose spiteful without joy,
I'm a good woman who's in need of more,
He lost sight when his wife got bored,
They're in a place, he didn't have a grip;
I'm satisfied, she missed that trip,
Just waiting, give me an excuse;
The space wasn't filled; he got real loose,
She heard the news, but he started to cry;
He showed weakness and we all knew why,
He was a boy, but she needed a man;
His wife won't mind, she'll understand,
They were together and had big plans;
He gave his time, I made no demands,
He's all worked up, who started the fight?
I'm dressed nice, it's a party tonight,
He got wasted, he walked home;
She got in trouble, she was left alone,
The man was free, he didn't want nobody;
She made a fuss, and we got real rowdy,
She had a gun, we didn't see that coming;
It was hot, so I took off running;

THE ERUPTION

Her man's dead, but I'm not talking;
She's looking hard, but mines still walking,
She turned around, but no one's left;
Now I'm standing strong all by myself.

Rock Stable...

Let me introduce you to someone I love,
She's a woman with all possibilities;
And I'm living only to meet her needs,
When I fulfill her destiny, then she'll be pleased,
God allowed the heavens to float down to me;
With a bit of greatness for you to see,
Relax and roll with her inspirations;
Until we reach our destination,
Listen closely and you'll be inspired;
All this talent, "This girls on fire!"
Now I thank God for all that is blessed;
The doors were empty, it was just a test,
Her beauty is full, she's not alone;
She spends her days singing a song,
Give me her thoughts and I'll send her mine;
Our thoughts together make one of a kind,
She's on that ship sailing through;
I caught in time, I saw her too,
Grab her joy, hold on tight;
She's up floating through the night,
It's sure to keep you satisfied;
The pleasure is sensational, you won't be denied,
Welcome to the world of good;
I'll label her flavor if I could,
Snatch her, catch her, she's all mine;

THE ERUPTION

I hope you are able to recognize,
As we press on for success;
I'm offering you my very best,
You'll get it all with christian values;
It was never meant to deprive you,
So, buckle up tight for the road;
Us together gonna rock your soul.

Jacqueline James

Time Out...

It was late in the afternoon;
When she tried to leave the room,
You can scream and you can shout;
But you're not getting out,
The time had come to pass;
Her best efforts didn't last,
Her attempts were wearing down;
So she needs to come around,
She was getting very bored;
And I was starting to get annoyed,
So I sat her down in a chair;
Trying hard to convince her,
That it was just a waste of time;
Now I'm about to lose my mind,
I told her that she had to stay;
But it wasn't for the entire day,
She got up and began to jump;
In return it made me stomp,
Then she said that she needed a bath;
And we both started to laugh,
She said that she was small and I was large;
And that's the only reason that I'm in charge,
I tried hard to keep my peace;
But she's a hyper little niece,

THE ERUPTION

I told her that she was in time out!
And that's what this is really all about,
In spite of what she heard;
She wasn't listening to a word,
Then she starts to kick the walls;
And you can hear it down the hall,
I asked her to settle down;
But she still continue to clown,
Then I told her that it was late in the afternoon;
And she'll be leaving soon,
So stop jumping about;
Because you're in time out!

Money… Money…

Rolling in the dough;
While on the go,
Counting that paper;
After during hard labor,
Stacking that cash;
Hoping it'll last,
Get that money;
Ain't nothing funny,
Got that gold;
Get it sold,
Diamonds are in;
Pawn them my friend,
It's your duty;
To get that ruby,
You'll get an opal;
If you're hopeful,
You'll have it made;
If you get that jade,
You got the world;
If you got a pearl,
It's a great symbol;
When you get an emerald,

THE ERUPTION

If you're going to shiver;
Then get some silver,
You can stop her;
If you get some copper,
Now that's how the story goes;
Whatever it is, it will be sold.

Party...

Dressed in all colors and in all styles;
Dancing on the stage for awhile,
Some in stripes some in plaid,
Some in dresses, others in pants,
We've all come out to have a good time,
Drinking gin and juice or vodka with lime,
Some had rum mixed with coke;
Some had beer like common folk,
Whatever drink was in your glass;
You drank it slow and made it last,
Some were slipping wine to pass the time;
Others just had a pop, but that was fine,
Either way we came out to party;
To dance and rock until the morning,
Some wore funky boots, some wore slides;
We all dressed up and went outside,
Some dance and some sang;
Others sat back and enjoyed the screen,
Some of us were tall, some were short;
Some of us were big, some were small;
But we all knew how to boogie-down,
Some of us were black and others white;
But we all came to a party for the night,

THE ERUPTION

We had a good time, we got real loose;
We party so hard, we made no excuse,
My feet were hurting, my legs were tried;
But I kept the party going on the Eastside,
I danced, I rocked, I felt great;
I danced until it got real late,
I got real funky and I got bold;
I stepped in line because I got soul!
I didn't mind the crowd, I didn't mind the view;
I danced even harder when saw you,
The band was live, up in the place;
The crowd cheered with smiles on their face,
We didn't get off the dance floor;
Until they turned off the lights and closed the door.

Me Time...

This is my best friend who wants to stay;
She came to be with me along the way,
She needs to go on and leave me alone;
I love her dearly, but I just have to roam,
I'm not going to let her cramp my style;
I'm going to sneak away for a while,
She means well, I'm sure of that;
But, I need some space and that's a fact,
She needs to hover over someone else;
I need some time for myself,
I know she's looking out for me and that's alright;
Cause we've been best friends our entire life,
She knows I need to be free so I can live;
So, a little privacy she needs to give,
I have to wonder and explore;
If I stay with her, it'll be a bore,
She'll always be my closest friend;
But right now, my time, I'm not going to lead!

THE ERUPTION

In The...

In the hay..why don't you to stay;
In the loo..you know what to do;
In the John ...stop messing around;
On the throne...now don't you rome;
In your spot...now don't you stop;
In the potty...you gotta get it outta you;
In the can...I hope you ran;
In the outhouse...can't go without;
In the office...stop that talking;
On the pot...now that was a lot;
In the room...it's coming soon;
On the toilet...you just farted;
In the bathroom...it's late afternoon.

Spicy Seniors...

Some of our seniors are busy indeed;
They're very spicy and full of greed,
I went with them to the races, to place a bet,
They pushed me so hard, off went my hat,
One of my earrings hit the floor;
A lady shouted, "That's not yours!"
A different woman picked it up;
But when I asked for it, she said, "Shut up!"
I wasn't sure just what to do;
So I showed her that it was the mate from two,
She gave it back with attitude;
But everyone seen, she was being rude,
I went to the buffet to eat my food;
Cause it was getting late in the afternoon,
I wanted to sit and eat at the table;
I squeezed between two when I was able,
They knocked each other over to get a spot;
And it didn't matter if they were handicap or not,
They say whatever comes out their mouths, without any tact;
They have no filters, and that's a fact,
They talk bad to each other all day long;
But at the end of the day, no one felt wronged,
They stick close to each other, their circles are full;

THE ERUPTION

They all have issues and that's for sure,
They're minds are sharp, they're very wise;
They have lots of knowledge, you'll be surprised,
Some walk stiff and may even fall,
When you talk about one, you talk about them all,
Some use canes and walkers, but that's okay;
Because they get where they need to be at the end of the day,
If they hitched a ride or drive a car;
They accept each other for who they are,
They laugh, joke, and have a good time;
Their bouts are harmless, that you'll find,
They all came to win lots of money;
And if get in their way, you're in for trouble,
Most of them retired from all different walks;
Some were bankers, teachers, and even cops;
Some were housewives or widowers who never worked;
Others were mechanics, secretaries, or even store clerks,
It doesn't make a difference what they did when they were young;
They're all spicy seniors now who came out for fun!

JACQUELINE JAMES

Old Folks...

They sit around and talk about their children if any;
And their grandchildren if many,
Others talk about family members and friends;
Or relatives who live in,
But they all talk about their body parts;
From the gray in their head to their bad heart,
They speak of the cataracts in their eyes;
To the cellulite in their thighs,
They talk about their loose flabby arms;
And that their shapes have no form;
They talk about how they have age spots on their face;
And how their big in the waist,
They talk about the wrinkles in their skin;
To their sagging extra chin,
They talk about the pain in their back;
To the leaks from their cracks,
They talk about their bad knees;
And how they can't walk with ease,
They talk about the gout in their legs,
And how they wet their bed,
They talk about their indigestion;
Then, they compare their suggestions,
They talk about their acid reflux;

THE ERUPTION

And the gas from their guts,
They talk about their kidneys and their bladders;
And that's all that really matters,
They speak of their body parts that don't work;
And the other ones that just hurt,
They talk about when their bowels lose control;
And how their pants gets a full load,
They talk about the arthritis in their limbs;
To ointments they use on them,
They talk about their cramps in their hands;
And, how its hard to meet life demands,
Oh let's not forget those tired feet;
They complain to everyone they greet,
How their ankles are swollen, their heels are tired;
And if they stand up too long, their blood pressure rise,
They talk about the pain that's all over;
And how it's just hard to maneuver,
They talk about how their skin is so dry;
And when the sun hits it, they fry,
They talk about the crook in their neck;
To the hump in their sack,
They talk about the sounds they can't hear;
To the things they now fear;
And they talk about the thoughts they can't find;
That was once in their mind,
Old folks will surely give you a laugh,
When they talk about the things on their behave.

Chapter 6

Special Dedication
1. Time to Heal...
2. Gone Home...
3. The King Called Me Home...
4. Liked Spirits...
5. R.I.P...

THE ERUPTION

Time to Heal...

I know you wanted desperately to commit to him, your life;
In spite of his indiscretions you were a loyal wife,
Regardless of the circumstances he didn't abide by any rules;
Nevertheless, it still broke your heart
when you were given the bad news,
Sometimes we're cut the deepest by ones we truly love;
But your healing will come from Our Father up above,
No ones here to disregard your feelings;
But right now it's time to get comfort through God's healing,
Your road to come may be challenging and hard;
But fight the good fight with God's word as your sword,
Your heart is broken, but don't allow it to become hardened;
God is here for you to make sure that your deeds are rewarded,
He'll give you peace in your time of sorrow, and grief;
So keep your trust in Jesus, you'll be blessed for your beliefs,
I know there is never enough solace, when the pain is piercing you;
Allow God to direct your path and you'll know exactly what to do,
Now I say to you with love today,
through your faith there's no restrictions;
Continue to keep God in the heart, and honor his words
with strong conviction,
Peace be still and know you're safe;
And may God bless you through His grace.

Jacqueline James

Gone Home...

God has blessed this precious life;
To become a mother, an aunt,
a sister, a cousin, a friend, and a wife,
We've come to that final hour;
When she's gone to meet the Lord, our father,
I know this may be difficult for our family to understand;
However, it's in God's perfect plan,
We want to remember the best from her;
How she loved us and showed how much she cared,
She was loving and kind with gentle ways;
God has giving her peace, in her final days,
We all know how sweet she was,
And how she was blessed through Jesus love,
The kindness she showed overwhelmed us all;
And, she remained humble when Jesus called,
The days she spent on this earth;
Will leave a remarkable glow from an Angel's worth,
It was truly an honor to have met her presence;
She taught me a lot through life's great lessons,
She'll be greatly missed and her memories cherished,
Especially how she fought the
fight with strength and showed courage,
Right now were weeping and filled with sorrow;
But with God's grace joy will come tomorrow,

THE ERUPTION

Now go ahead and dry your eyes;
We're just here to say our final goodbyes,
Her body may return to the dirt;
However her spirit's with Jesus, from her good works,
May God reign comfort over her family;
As we trust that she's at peace resting in heaven,
In Loving Memories
Reatha Gene Whitehorn
(2-1-1945)-(7-27-17)

Jacqueline James

The King Called Me Home...

Please don't look for me, I'm gone;
The King has called me home!
He said, "Well done my faithful servant,"
Because of my faithfulness, I deserved it,
My time I spent on earth was good;
But it was up, I thought you'd understand;
I'm no longer sick, nor am I in pain;
My Lord and Savior, has called my name;
I'll be missed, but it's okay;
I miss you guys as well, but I couldn't stay,
Just remember me, when you pray,
I know that you love me and I love you guys as well,
However I'm up in heaven right now and
boy do I have a story to tell,
I'm no longer in pain, nor am I crying;
I'm at so much peace and I'm doing fine,
It's so beautiful up here, God saved a place for me;
Just keep your faith and wait your turn and you'll be able to see,
But as of now, you'll must stay cause
it's plenty of work to be done;
You must tell the world about God's love
and teach them about his son!

THE ERUPTION

You must tell everyone about the bible stories;
How we serve a forgiving God and there's no need to worry,
Because of God's mercy and his grace;
I could see my Father's face!
Please don't cry for me while I'm not there for you to see;
I'm exactly where I need to be,
I'll always be with you even though I'm gone;
Just cherish my memories in your heart and take me along,
In Loving Memories
Reatha Gene Whitehorn
(2-1-1945)-(7-27-17)

Liked Spirits...

Like spirits attract each other;
Even if they are from different mothers,
Our Father is the same from the beginning to the end,
Now our paths have crossed to remain friends;
Our chains have linked and there's a reason why;
You're an artist and so am I,
God has blessed us with a very special gift;
To give him the glory as our voices lift,
I thank God right now for putting you in my life;
You're a beautiful person and I'm sure an amazing wife,
So as you continue to do the work for the Lord;
I'm praying for peace so your burdens aren't hard,
May you prosper throughout your test;
And may God be with you and continue to bless.

Dedicated to: Sister Marilynn Dunn
;

THE ERUPTION

R.I.P...

Andre Jones was a husband, father, son,
brother, cousin, and friend,
None of us wanted his life to end,
We're all gathered here today to acknowledge him,
His soul that will continue to live;
Because we serve a mighty God whose always willing to forgive,
Although I did not know him, I met him passing by;
His soul has left his body to be with our Father in the sky,
His body is no longer with us and shall never return again;
But he is resting in peace because he has Jesus as his friend,
His time here on earth was cut way too short;
Well keep his precious memories buried in our heart,
He was given time to repent from any unpleasant ways;
God has called him home to give him brighter days,
Now he's occupying one of God's many rooms;
And after our time here expires we'll meet with him again soon,
Sometimes in our lives we only get one season;
In spite of all the issues God has his own reasons,
We may not understand the events that took place;
But we must keep our faith in Jesus to see our Father's face,
After we lose a loved one we're all left in sorrow;
We'll mourn the life that once was but joy will come tomorrow,

So go ahead a cry for the life we all loved;
And trust he's resting peacefully with our Father up above,
In Loving Memories, Andre Jones
(9-14-88)--(5-25-17)

THE ERUPTION

Jacqueline James